The Lost Railway Li⌐

Contents

Foreword

Portpatrick, Whithorn and Garlieston were wiped off the rail map when I was in my teens, but I shall always regret not having taken later opportunities to travel over other Galloway routes. It was bad planning, through not checking the timetable, which led me to miss a train at Dumfries minutes after it had left for Castle Douglas and the west. Not only did I miss a train that day, but I also missed an opportunity of a life-time, for soon afterwards the line was closed and the rails were lifted.

Those of us who grew up in the 1950s and 1960s enjoyed a golden age of leisure. Full employment, rising wages and longer holidays gave us the opportunity to travel widely and purchase our own form of transport. Even in my second hand car I was able to reach the north of Scotland or the Lake District quicker than by using the less flexible public transport available. The Galloway Hills were now only an hour or so away and it was no longer necessary to decamp for an annual fortnight's holiday to be able to explore an area.

Trains were an added attraction to the landscape in those days, and as I hurried to the hills I was always promising myself 'rest' days when I would sit back in a rail carriage and see the scenery from a new angle.

The hills are still around today, but alas, the trains have vanished from Galloway save for the lines north from Stranraer and Dumfries at the edges of the region. Nothing remains in the centre except for features of the permanent way, which become less and less permanent every year as they gradually decay, and Nature takes over.

We quickly forget where once trains ran, and are only reminded by sight of an occasional embankment, a converted station building, the abutments of a bridge, or, more rarely, a still standing viaduct.

4

THE LOST RAILWAY LINES

OF GALLOWAY

Alasdair Wham

A series of journeys along the many disused railway routes in Galloway. Lines that have closed and now pass, silent through countryside and town. These are journeys into the recent past with an eye on what remains today. Explore and discover the heritage that the railway era has left behind.

Proceeds from this book are being donated to Barcaple Christian Outdoor Centre, Ringford, near Castle Douglas, Kirkcudbrightshire DG7 2AP.

THE LOST RAILWAY LINES OF GALLOWAY

Alasdair Wham

Dedicated to.
Christine,
Neil, Iain, Martin and Scott

Illustrations by Kay Stevenson

ISBN 1 872350 96 8

Published and typeset by:
G.C. BOOK PUBLISHERS LTD., North Main Street,
Wigtown, Scotland

Cover photographs; The Big Water-of-Fleet Viaduct
& inset Loch Ken Viaduct
Alasdair Wham

Acknowledgements

My thanks to Christine for her help in checking the text; to Neil for his companionship on the walks and for his willingness to help with researching the background information; to Ken and Sheena Andrew whose encouragement and interest in the project I greatly valued; to Allan Phin, Editor, 'Galloway News' for encouraging me by publishing my articles; to Kay Stevenson for illustrating the text and to Chris Hendry for his help.

It is this landscape which Alasdair Wham explores. We cannot turn the clock back and recreate a railway system as it was. But we can walk with him over historical routes which once gave service to the nation. Railwaymen and their womenfolk devoted their lives to staffing stations and signal boxes, and running trains for our benefit. It was not their fault if we did not turn up, or turned up too late. The chance of making these journeys by rail has gone for the present under the harsh fiscal policies of remote governments.

History may yet condemn the motor car to oblivion as it has all but done with the steam locomotive, and new forms of transport may evolve to serve Galloway and elsewhere in the future. No matter what the future holds, we shall always need to exercise our legs, bodies and minds.

Exploring redundant rail routes is an excellent form of recreation, and I commend this book to readers for the effort and research that went into it, and the stimulation it offers for exercise in normally hidden parts of Galloway's splendid landscape.

Ken Andrew

Introduction

Hanging eighty feet above the ground on an abseiling rope was a new and not entirely enjoyable experience. Despite assurances, the instructors from the Outdoor Centre had not totally convinced me that I could make it to the bottom of the old railway viaduct . The viaduct spanned the Big Water -of-Fleet in the Galloway Hills some six miles from Gatehouse-of-Fleet and about two miles from the site of the now closed Gatehouse-of-Fleet Station. The white faces of the members of my Bible Class suggested that they shared similar concerns as they awaited their turn, and determined not to yield to my fears I tried to force my mind to think of anything but the descent. I knew little about the viaduct other than I thought that it featured briefly in John Buchan's, 'The 39-Steps'. As I began my slow descent, I wondered about the history of the railway lines which ran through such wild and beautiful countryside.

Later safely on solid ground and back at the Barcaple Christian Outdoor Centre near Ringford in the Tarff Valley, where our group were spending an activity weekend I asked one of the instructors about the history of the railway line. He told me that there were many old railways in the area and looking across the valley he pointed out nestling in the side of the hill, Tarff Station which had been part of the Castle Douglas to Kirkcudbright branch. A story about a runaway train which didn't stop at the buffers in Kirkcudbright but continued across the road and into the unfortunate Mr Patterson's house made me curious to learn more about the railways in this area. This was my introduction to the railways that used to run through Galloway.

Shortly afterwards I discovered that Ken Andrew, well-known author and photographer, had walked the route of the disused railway from Dumfries to Challoch Junction, in 1974 when I read his article 'Westwards Through Galloway', originally published in'The Scots Magazine'. I then extended my walks to include the other disused lines in the area and to repeat his journey twenty years on.

Many of the articles in this book have been published previously in the 'Galloway News', but this is the first time that they have appeared as a collection. I have reworked many of the articles to include extra information and to avoid jargon so that the articles will appeal to those who know little about railways but want to learn about the countryside of South-West Scotland, while hopefully still appealing to the railway enthusiast.

To anyone committed to rail transport, much of what I have written must make bleak reading. Nothing, however, stands still and when the railways closed, nature and man attacked - slowly in some areas, faster in others. The hopes of the railway builders have not survived the economic and political realities of another century.

However, maybe the arrogance of the railway builders had something to do with their eventual demise. In an era when there was little competition it didn't matter that many stations were inconveniently sited, but when choice appeared in the form of cars and buses their flexibility meant that the railways were less likely to be used. Even that wouldn't have necessarily meant the end if the railways could have focused on what they were good at – transporting goods and people long distances. But a crippling lack of vision and inability to promote the attractions of the line for the importance of its links to Ireland meant that the age of the train was always going to be brief.

Sadly this lack of foresight continued when the railways closed. The routes would have been ideal for long-distance walkways or even local walks. Little was done and now the disused lines are showing signs of fading away. In ten years it is unlikely that the Big Water-of-Fleet Viaduct will survive and probably not many of the others viaducts. The routes of the lines will have been lost, but not forgotten. The memories of the railway age remain strong in Galloway.

A word of caution, however, since the railways closed it is not always clear who owns the land. In many areas I suspect that British Rail have sold the land to local landowners and farmers. I would advise you to seek the permission of the landowner where possible and to follow the Country Code. Please do not assume that because a walk is described in this book that anyone has given permission for you to follow in my footsteps. It is also important to keep off dangerous and disused structures, such as viaducts which have been closed to the public.

I hope that you will enjoy the journeys along the lost lines.

Alasdair Wham,
Ayr,
January, 1996

Journey A

Walking the Paddy Line Today

From Dumfries to Castle Douglas

The start of the Port Road

This journey really started at a road bridge over the main railway line in Dumfries. Looking towards the south, Dumfries Railway Station and engine shed could be seen. The mainline to Glasgow stops here and then continues north under the bridge. Turning and looking the other way the route continues north and while the track layout has changed, a branch line still veers left. This is where the Port Road once began its long and winding journey to Portpatrick a distance of eighty miles. Along this line through Galloway, ran the famous 'Paddies' the trains which connected with the boats to Ireland.

9

The track still crosses the River Nith and continues over the Garroch Viaduct, but just beyond there, nearly three miles from where it started, it now stops at the ICI factory at Maxwellton, where there was a station on the outskirts of Dumfries. Sadly the line is now truncated. The steel artery that once carried people and goods back and forwards through Galloway and linked to Ireland has been severed, because the line that enters the ICI factory, never leaves it.

The first part of the Port Road route started as a branch line between Dumfries and Castle Douglas, when the Castle Douglas and Dumfries Railway opened in 1859, but became more significant with the opening of the Portpatrick Railway(PPR) two years later in 1861 which completed the route to the coast. Within twenty years the line which had been built as single track was made double track, to cope with the extra business generated by the opening of the PPR. Just over a hundred years later the Beeching cuts closed all the lines between Maxwellton and Challoch Junction, where the line from Girvan used to link with the Portpatrick Railway.

Now thirty years later, we were about to follow in the steps of the Paddy and trace what remained of the Port Road today. Our walk started, therefore, at Drumsleet near the ICI works where the sandstone abutments of a railway bridge stand to each side of the old military road. Carefully avoiding our first obstacle, a garden allotment which had taken over the first few yards, we strode out along the disused line. Passing through pleasant countryside we quickly left the ICI works behind, before entering a deep cutting hewn from solid rock which eventually emerged at the Goldielea viaduct. A wire fence blocked our progress but did not hide the tall graceful structure, consisting of ten semi-circular masonry spans. Although partly hidden from the road, it dwarfed the nursing home which nestled at its foot, from which the viaduct took its name. Taller than the more famous Big-Water-of-Fleet viaduct it remained in good condition despite the trees which grew from its ballast. To avoid the detour we had to make, it might be better to join the disused track after the viaduct but first pause to pay your respects to this grand old viaduct which is largely ignored by the traffic whizzing past on the nearby road.

Beyond the viaduct, the line ran alongside the A711 for several miles. Likewise, here, travellers along the road might not even be aware of the route's existence, due to bushes and trees blocking their view down to the track, which ran in a deep cutting. Costs for this section were understandably very high due to the heavy earthworks required to construct the cuttings. Now the line is used only by farmers and at one point as a storage for trucks. An overhead power line follows the disused route.

The line eventually emerged at a road bridge at the site of Lochanhead Station, into a wide valley, six miles from Dumfries. An early closure, the original station building now converted into a dwelling-house remains along with the faint traces of railway sidings to the east. Like many stations on this line it must have been built for the railway's convenience as there is no population to support it and only a few farms to feed produce to it.

After Lochanhead Station the line reached open countryside filled with fields of cattle, with Bengairn and Screel hills visible in the distance. Until Kirkgunzeon the railway kept to the north side of the A711. After a walk of over two miles the remains of Killywhan Station was reached, situated about half-a-mile to the northwest of the little village of Beeswing, on the west side of a minor road. Given the number of people who lived in this part of the valley, many a train driver must have watched in vain for potential passengers, coming from this small village resting in the shade of Lotus Hill, to catch the train. There was a level crossing just to the east of the station. The original station building, now an attractive house extended since its railway days, still existed with its long platform intact.

After this point the line did a vanishing trick for the next two miles, the track having been reclaimed by the local farmer and ploughed into the fields, apart from a cottage for a level-crossing keeper near Drumjohn. The line was not visible again until just before Kirkgunzeon Station when an old road bridge over the line indicated its return. A thick wooden log replaced what must have been a small railway bridge before a muddy field is crossed leading to the Station itself which was now a caravan park. Caravans stretch out where before trains must have waited patiently for passengers from Kirkgunzeon village a quarter of-a-mile away to the north.

Beyond Kirkgunzeon the route was overgrown for a hundred yards as it approached the A711. The line then reappeared on the south side of the A711, the rail bridge having been lost to road realignment, before heading up the other side of the valley towards woods where we knew that the next station, Southwick was situated. This was one of the most pleasant stretches with outstanding views to the north over the valley. The line was largely left untouched occupied only by sheep although beside a small loch, not marked on my edition of the Ordnance Survey map the local angling club have a caravan parked on a bridge over a burn. Here I spotted what I thought were two planes circling over the hills but on focusing my binoculars on them one plane turned out to be an eagle (or perhaps a buzzard) soaring high above!

From this high point the line headed down towards Southwick. Here the woods have closed in on the site of the station forming an unpleasant and almost impenetrable swamp. We had to leave the line and cut round by what was once cottages used by railway workers and which was now a private residence. We followed a forestry track until by chance the remains of the station platform were spotted hidden among bushes and trees. Little is recognisable of what was once a busy station complete with signal box and footbridge, with trains delivering workers to the nearby munitions works at Edingham Moss. Strands of rusting fences indicated the start of the once secret munitions factory built during the war, which made gun cotton for the ICI factory at Powfoot. Sunken buildings surrounded by high banks of sand to contain explosions are scattered around the countryside now only occupied by rabbits (many of which were black) and a few cows. There were signs of extensive sidings and for half-a-mile another disused railway embankment ran parallel. The wood was now far behind. At the end of a long stretch, a transport company have taken over some of the old buildings and added some of their own. A strong steel linked fence meant a detour and the course of the line was further broken up by a new road built across it.

Siding at Edingham Moss

Finally we regained the line which now led into another deep cutting which slowly curved round a small hill and into the

13

outskirts of Dalbeattie. Here the route all but disappeared with the rail bridge demolished and on the other side of where the bridge once stood a row of new houses followed the line of the old railway. All that remained of the station was an old engine shed the rest of the area being occupied by disused factories. It is hard to imagine that the railway ever ran through this attractive granite town whose prosperity was based on the quarries which lay to the south-east of the town. Granite from Dalbeattie as well as giving a distinctive appearance to many of the town's buildings has been exported far and wide by rail and sea. Many important buildings in London and elsewhere are built of Dalbeattie granite. There was no sign of the aerial ropeway which once carried crushed stone from the nearby quarry to a loading bay next to the railway, a distance of about half-a-mile and which carried 200 tons a day.

The route was again recognisable on the other side of the B794 and from there the line ran towards the Urr Water. Just before the bridge was the site of the worst accident on this part of the line which occurred in 1874 when a ballast train and a Caledonian train collided just a hundred yards before the bridge. The line which was single track at this time was operating a 'staff' and ticket system. The idea being that the 'staff' was needed to open a locked box and get a ticket which gave authorisation to proceed. The ballast train had the staff but a Caledonian train fed up with waiting, persuaded an assistant in the absence of the Station Master, who had gone into town on Company business, to give them a ticket to proceed. Of course he shouldn't have been able to do this but it turned out that a standard issue poker could operate the locked box as well as the 'staff'. Three people died.

Stone pillars were all that remained of the bridge over the Urr. The first bridge had been washed away, the second consisting of two bowstring girder spans was built so strong, that it took four months to dismantle when the railway closed. A pleasant paddle on a hot day took us across the river where the track swung north around hills. The railway slowly climbed at this point with an increasing panorama over the Urr valley, with the distinctive shape of the Motte of Urr drawing closer and further to the north-west the village of the Haugh of Urr. We found what we thought were the remains of the earliest station to close on the line. Buittle Halt was closed a hundred years ago. Only one train a week each way, which was on a Wednesday afternoon ever stopped here. A few yards on evidence of sidings were still discernible beside a dismantled railway bridge.

The track now started to swing west towards Castle Douglas before eventually reaching the A745 at the site of a bridge which once took the railway over the old road. The line was lost now, symbolically, to the realigned road. No sign of the track was found until near the boundary of Castle Douglas.

Stone Pillars – Bridge over the Urr

Castle Douglas, once an important rail centre and still the market-town for the area has also succeeded in removing most traces of its station. Like Dalbeattie, only an old engine shed still stands along with parts of the platform, in the industrial estate which now occupied the site.

The first part of our journey showed that much of the line remained in the countryside and long stretches could be walked. In the towns, however, the pressure for building space had succeeded in many of the remnants of the railway being lost. There was no doubt that what would have been a sleepy rural branch line was transformed by its connection to the Portpatrick Railway. The Castle Douglas and Dumfries Railway would have been a possible early candidate for closure, if the plans to connect Castle Douglas and Portpatrick had not materialised.

Stations and main features (mileage from Dumfries)

A1　Dumfries Station: 0 miles (84) 977 765

A2　Garroch Viaduct: 2.25 miles (still in use) (84) 947 751

A3　Drumsleet: 3 miles (start of walk) (84) 944 743

A4　Goldielea Viaduct: 4 miles (closed) (84) 931 735

A5　Lochanhead Station:　6 miles (private residence)
　　　(84) 916 717

A6　Killywhan Station: 8.5 miles (private residence)
　　　(84) 889 694

A7　Kirkgunzeon Station: 10.5 miles (caravan park)
　　　(84) 872 664

A8　Southwick Station: 12.5 miles (now in the middle of a wood next to site of former Edingham Munitions works)
　　　(84) 856 634

A9　Dalbeattie Station: 14.5 miles (site occupied by a disused factory) (84) 833 617

A10　Urr bridge:　15.5 miles (now dismantled) (84) 822 626

A11　Buittle Halt: 17 miles (site of) (84) 812 641

A12　Castle Douglas Station: 20 miles (site occupied by garage and Station Yard industrial estate) (84) 768 628

Journey B

The Line That Stopped At Bob Patterson's Door

The Kirkcudbright Branch

Talk of a railway to Kirkcudbright had been discussed for many years and as early as 1845 a route had been surveyed with the hope that the railway to Portpatrick would pass through the town taking a coastal route via Gatehouse-of-Fleet. When these plans were abandoned it was quickly decided to establish a branch line to Kirkcudbright. Construction of the single track line, ten and a quarter miles in length, with no tunnels and only a few bridges caused no major problems and was completed within three years.

A dispute, however, caused by the junction of the Kirkcudbright line with the Portpatrick line, only three hundred yards from Castle Douglas Station caused delays to the opening of the line for passengers although it was opened for freight on the 17th February, 1864. The railway inspector wanted a double line of rails at this point for safety reasons before permitting passengers and the Portpatrick Railway Company(PPR) would not agree.

To enable passengers to use the line to Castle Douglas, a temporary station was built at Abercromby Road near Carlingwark Moss to the south of the town, called St Andrews Station. The Kirkcudbright line was thus opened to passengers as far as this station and the service began on the 7th March 1864 with passengers being conveyed to Castle Douglas's other station, by horse drawn omnibus. Later that year, after a further inspection, passengers were able to travel the last three hundred yards as long as the speed of the train did not exceed 5mph.

Behind both the CD&DR and the Kirkcudbright

Railways(KR) was the mighty hand of the Glasgow and South-West Railway (GSWR) who had funded both railways and a year later took them into complete ownership. Not wanting to pay running fees to the PPR they constructed a new route over the disputed junction. While St Andrews Station was only temporary, probably wooden in structure, it is still shown 30 years later on the Ordnance Survey map of 1895.

Arriving in Castle Douglas on a grey, overcast Sunday afternoon, my son Neil and I set out to explore the town and to identify the site of the stations and the route that the railway took. Nowadays it is difficult to trace the route. The main station site near the cattle market is occupied by an industrial estate, with only one of the original engine sheds, now converted to a builders' merchant and part of the old platform remaining. The road bridge under which the trains left for Stranraer and Kirkcudbright is filled in and the junction of the two railways (KR and PPR) is landscaped and now a park. The KR branched to the left at this point parting from the mainline. At the edge of the park housing has been built along the line of the railway although there is still a path which winds through the estate closely following the route and ending at a road bridge where the road to Ayr crosses the old line. A metal barrier stops you passing under the bridge. It was here that St Andrews Station was sited, although no trace remains. To the town side of the bridge an imposing stone and brick building, now converted into four substantial terrace houses, was built as 'The Station Hotel'. The present station hotel in Castle Douglas was at that time known as the Temperance Hotel and is beside the site of the former mainline station.

Standing on the bridge, the line of the railway can be clearly seen for a few hundred yards, overgrown with nettles and wild raspberry canes running between housing and the golf course. The route of the railway towards Carlingwark Moss is

18

further interrupted by a sewage works and the golf course and the last bridge in the town is filled in. Beyond that a car scrapyard obliterates the route. Thus, in the nearly thirty years since the line was closed little remains of the railway. Even the Castle Douglas town trail leaflet wrongly identifies which railway took this route, claiming mistakenly that this was the route followed by the Stranraer to Dumfries line. The railways, which were greeted with such enthusiasm, have in little more than a hundred years disappeared from the town!

Next morning with little improvement in the weather, we set out to follow the route of the line from Castle Douglas. Starting where the line crossed Carlingwark Moss a natural obstacle with poor drainage which the builders of the line overcame by raising the track several feet above the surrounding ground - we headed out in the direction of the fairly recently opened by-pass which cuts across the path of the line. Reaching Carlingwark Lane, which was once a canal linking Carlingwark Loch to the River Dee and is now a deep drainage ditch we found that a bridge had been removed and Neil and I were forced to pick our way carefully over the muddy ground to the by-pass. Tracing the line from here was difficult, and our spirits began to sag as the line on the far side of the by-pass had been ploughed into the fields. However we spotted the track of the old line hugging the side of a small hill. Here the line has been used as a dump and we had to work our way carefully through the rubbish pausing for the last time to look back at Castle Douglas. Hearing the sound of the town bells, we turned away before we rounded the hill and came to a road bridge which carries a narrow road over the old railway line leading to Kelton Mains Farm and the beginning of the Threave Wildfowl Refuge. Visitors can park their cars at the farm before walking the zig-zag path to the boat which carries them to Threave Castle.

At last, the walking became pleasant and we noticed that

some work had been done to use the line as a walkway. We wandered through the many trees, mainly birch and willow, which have grown tall and spindly searching for the light out of the railway bed. Unfortunately, as they grow, trees often block the drainage and the ground became muddy underfoot. Looking through the trees and bushes which grew to each side of the old track we could see cattle and sheep grazing and sometimes intruding onto the line where the wire fence had snapped. After about half-a-mile we found built into the side of the track a wooden hide with peep holes for bird-watchers to use to observe the greylag geese in winter, or the many other birds which are found in this area. A little further and we reached the River Dee where the railway crossed the river by the clever use of a small island, and two girder bridges, only the first of which still stands. The island, heavily wooded is also used as part of the nature reserve. Care has to be taken not to disturb the birds that refuge here and the warden should be contacted. On the far side, only the pillars of the second bridge remain as the railway reaches out two hundred yards towards the Bridge of Dee Station.

Bridge of Dee Station

20

To reach the station we had to detour to the A75 and cross the Threave Bridge before taking the minor road to Netherhall where we quickly regained the railway at a bridge beside the Bridge of Dee Station. The station is situated only a few hundred yards from the village of the same name which lies on the other side of the A75 and consisted of a single building and platform with a small goods yard to the west. The station was closed in 1949 and was in a very derelict state before it became a private residence. The station building has been restored and the gardens well landscaped with clear signs of the original platform remaining. We spent an enjoyable time talking to the owner whose permission we had sought before examining the old station.

Now at nearly three miles from Castle Douglas, the railway was passing through beautiful countryside with low rolling hills some topped with fields of golden barley, appearing luminous under the grey clouds which scurried overhead, and views to the north of Threave Castle sitting on an island in the River Dee. Looking around I could appreciate the reason why the station closed 15 years before the rest of the line given that it served so small a population.

The next part of our journey was uneventful - the line being well defined and only the roar of traffic from the nearby A75 spoiling the peace. Beyond the abutments of the bridge over the road to Glenlochar stands the concrete skeleton of another railway bridge like a fossilised memorial to the passing of the railway. From this point until close to the site of the old bridge over the A75 the walking is pleasant alongside conifers which knew nothing of the railway, growing rapidly as they do in so many parts of Galloway.

The line is lost for a while as the widened and re-routed A75 removes any trace of the line before it emerges on the other side at the site of some cattle pens. Here, as we climbed the side of the Tarff Valley, the sun broke through the layer of clouds brightening the valley and highlighting the village of Ringford and further to the west, the pyramidal shape of Neilson's Monument built in memory of the inventor of the hot blast method of smelting iron. Down in the valley we were aware of the scar created by the gas pipeline to Ireland nearly following the route that the railway planners had hoped in 1845 would carry the trains to Ireland.

It took us another half-hour to complete the slow climb towards Tarff Station which is almost seven miles from Castle Douglas. The station provided the only passing point on the railway and consisted of a single platform facing towards the hill and a goods yard. The stone station buildings, a mirror image of those at Bridge of Dee, provided accommodation for those climbing up from the valley below. As at Bridge of Dee a signal box was removed before the line closed.

Fossilised remains of old railway

Tarff is about seven miles from Gatehouse-of-Fleet, roughly the same distance from the town as the station known as Gatehouse-of-Fleet which existed on the Portpatrick Railway line. It seems that the owners of both lines wanted to name their stations after the town to attract business and so the owners of the KR changed the name of Tarff Station to Gatehouse-of-Fleet just one year after the station opened in 1864. At about the same time the name of the Gatehouse-of-Fleet Station on the PPR was changed to Dromore (the station is just beside the Clints of Dromore). A year later the name of this station was changed back from Dromore to Gatehouse-of-Fleet Station and both stations remained with that name until 1871 when the station on the KR was changed back to Tarff and the station on the PPR was changed to Dromore again (that is until 1912 when it reverted to Gatehouse-of-Fleet once more)!

Tarff Station

23

Tarff Station is now used by Tarff Valley Limited, originally set up in 1903 as a farmers' cooperative to buy supplies of coal and lime to be delivered by rail to the station. Gradually this company took over the station site until they purchased the whole property in 1966 two years after the station closed. The station building remains almost unchanged today, but is now surrounded by large sheds.

From here the line winds round Doon Hill with its views over the valley to Twynholm. The line then gradually descends towards Kirkcudbright which is soon spotted in the distance with its prominent Kirkcudbright Parish Church spire, previously St Cuthbert's Parish Church. On a summer's evening with the shadows lengthening, the views from the train must have been breathtaking. I could imagine the excitement created by travellers on the train with the first glimpse of their destination by the coast.

As we paused for lunch and to enjoy the view, we saw a succession of rain showers sweep in over Kirkcudbright and towards us. We were glad of the cover provided by the trees, which had seeded themselves on the line, as we sheltered from the rain. There was one unusual obstacle on this part of the line – a bee-hive which we carefully avoided!

Abruptly, as we moved closer to Kirkcudbright, the line stopped at an old bridge at which only one abutment remained. Beyond this no trace of the line remained, as it had been carefully ploughed into the fields until we reached the road. Here we found Telford's Road Bridge at Tongland, still impressive with its long central arch and the three flood arches to each side to allow for the 20 foot tidal surges. A few yards further up river we rediscovered the old railway, as we spotted the remains of the third and most spectacular railway bridge on this line over the River Dee. 'The Prince of Wales' viaduct completed in time for the marriage of the Prince and Princess of Wales on the 10th

24

March, 1863 with 58 foot high pillars of red sandstone, now without the metal girders which connected them, stand as impressive memorials of the skill of the railway builders. Two hundred yards up-river was the imposing facade of the white-walled Tongland Power Station.

While it is possible to regain the old track beyond the bridge on the Kirkcudbright side it became increasingly difficult for Neil and I to walk along as buildings have been built encroaching on the line. Eventually forced to walk along the road we spotted the landscaped remains of the rail bridge over the main road and knew we were only half-a-mile from the final station on the line. Of Kirkcudbright Station, which we reached mid-afternoon, only the ticket office remains, now converted into a shop. A housing estate is built on the rest of the site where there was a goods yard and a coal depot.

Remains of Tongland Viaduct

25

When the station was in use, only a buffer separated the railway from the main road. This was not the safest of arrangements as was shown in 1963 when a rear engined train descending from Tarff failed to stop, smashing through the buffer and across the main road, stopping at Mr Patterson's shop and house opposite. The carriage ended up twisted in the air. No one was hurt although the Station Master, Mr Maxwell who was also the Provost was none too pleased, however given that it was at the beginning of the Carnival Week the publicity did no harm. The humorous poem 'The Runaway train' captures the event. The station at Kirkcudbright had one other claim to fame and this was due to the Station Master, as from 1952 until 1964 the station won the best kept station garden award.

The Kirkcudbright line closed to passengers on the 3rd May, 1965 and it is not difficult to see why. If the mainline service from Dumfries to Stranraer could not survive Beeching, then a branchline had no chance! The line never generated enough business and only in wartime could it have been considered an important link when the line was busy transporting tanks to the nearby firing range. Sadly the line was in trouble as soon as the motor car became common on the Galloway roads, and without the foresight to promote it as a tourist attraction the line was doomed.

The Runaway Train

The runaway train came over the hill and she blew
The runaway train came over the hill and she blew
The runaway train came down by the Dee
And headed straight for the deep blue sea
And she blew.

The local inhabitants turned in their sleep as she blew
The local inhabitants turned in their sleep as she blew
The local inhabitants jumped to their feet
As the carriage charged across the street
And she blew.

Bob Patterson lay in his bed with a snore, as she blew
Bob Patterson lay in his bed with a snore, as she blew
Bob Patterson lay in his bed with a snore
But he jumped as the carriages banged his door
And she blew.

His daughters dreamed of the Carnival Ball as she blew
His daughters dreamed of the Carnival ball as she blew
His daughters dreamed of the Carnival Ball
And the buffer went right through the restaurant wall
And she blew.

The Porter stood with a smile of bliss as she blew
The Porter stood with a smile of bliss as she blew
He said as he stood with that smile of bliss
Castle Douglas had never a stunt like this
And she blew.

The Provost stood with his tongue in his cheek as she blew
The Provost stood with his tongue in his cheek as she blew
The Provost stood with his tongue in his cheek
And said 'What a start to the Carnival Week!'
And she blew.

ANON

Stations and other features (mileage from Castle Douglas)

B1   Castle Douglas Station: 0 miles, (84) 768 628
B2   St Andrews Station: 0.5 mile, (84) 763 623
B3   Bridge of Dee Station: 2.75miles, (84) 732 603
B4   Tarff Station: 6.75miles, (84) 686 564
B5   Tongland Bridge: 8.5 miles,
     (near Tongland Power Station) (84) 693 534
B6   Kirkcudbright Station: 10.25miles, (84) 686 512

Journey C

From Meadow to Moorland

Castle Douglas to Gatehouse-of-Fleet Station

Castle Douglas had once boasted of two railway stations and had shown great enthusiasm for the coming of the railways. The railway age arrived in Castle Douglas when the first train left for Dumfries on the 7th November, 1859 and soon the service on the Castle Douglas and Dumfries Railway(CD&DR) was so popular that extra trains were provided. When on the 12th March, 1861, the first train reached Castle Douglas from Stranraer (Portpatrick Railway), the town stopped being at the end of a branch and became a railway centre. The railway bridge was crowded with spectators as the town celebrated its new status. The Portpatrick line was now open and with it the route to Ireland.

From Castle Douglas to Gatehouse-of-Fleet Station along the disused Paddy Line is almost twenty miles. Yet within that distance, modest by inter-city standards, is a journey of stark contrasts, from the pleasant lochside meadows of Loch Ken, to the remote and rugged moorland of the hills round Loch Skerrow. The extensive planting of conifers has softened the moorland but the contrast is still there as the route of the disused railway climbs towards its summit near Gatehouse-of-Fleet Station.

Many were surprised that the Portpatrick and Wigtownshire Railway took the route north from Castle Douglas, and ignored the claims of those clamouring for the railway to head towards Kirkcudbright and then to Gatehouse-of-Fleet, thereafter keeping to the coast. Building costs were cheaper if the railway swung north and the Loch Ken route was finally favoured, after much argument. Hints that a link could be formed between the PPR and a route south from the Ayrshire coalfields via Dalmellington also might have played some part. The railway builders were nothing if not dreamers.

Castle Douglas, where we started our walk, is a town which has lost its connection with the railways. A tourist visiting would not know that the town once boasted two stations, albeit briefly, as all signs of the railways have been landscaped or built upon. (The second station, St Andrews Station is mentioned in the article on the Kirkcudbright Line.) The site of the former Castle Douglas Station is now occupied by a garage and the appropriately named Station Yard industrial estate and was situated next to the cattle market at the north end of the town.

As far as Crossmichael, there were only glimpses of the route taken by the former railway as it started its journey north on the east side of the A713. The route can be seen on the far side of Stewartry Rugby Club but what did remain was a jungle of nettles and brambles. At Drumskelly where the road used to

Crossmichael Station

twist over the railway, the road has been realigned and no remains of the road bridge could be seen. From this site until the station at Crossmichael there was no trace of the railway. The walker would be advised to take the bus to Crossmichael where the track can be rejoined at the site of the former station, which is down by the lochside towards the north end of the village. The platforms and building, now a private residence, were clearly identifiable. Even the signal box, although in a very dangerous state remains and the sidings to the north of the station can still be seen. From here until the station at Parton the line never strayed far from the lochside, carried on an embankment. The walking was pleasant and the route taken by the PPR almost intact for these three miles.

On the approach to Parton Station, the village, a scene of serenity with its distinctive terraced houses is dominated by the church on the right of the track and on the left the "pudding shaped" motte of Parton. The station building which is at the north end of the village has been extended as a private residence but still proudly bears its name. The platform remained but the

Maxwell Memorial

31

sidings were built upon. It is very probable that, one of the twenty most influential people who ever lived, according to a recent survey, used this tiny station on a regular basis. Who knows what the thoughts of James Clerk-Maxwell were as he approached the station on his return from Cambridge where he did most of his work. The stature of this most famous of scientists ranks beside Einstein as the founder of modern science. If the railway helped to ease his travels, then it justified its construction. We paused to pay our respects at the memorial stone outside the church to this scientist whose work led to radio, television and radar among other things.

After the railway left Parton it passed through a narrow cutting now designated by the local caravan park as a dog-walking trail, before swinging over the loch by the Loch Ken viaduct, its three rusting bowstring girders stretching over the loch at its narrowest point. The walker is now stopped, as the bridge is closed, its wooden planks too dangerous to ensure a safe passage. Apart from swimming there is no alternative, but to travel by road to Mossdale the site of New Galloway Station.

Loch Ken Viaduct

Here the determined walker can retrace his steps for one-and-a-half miles through gentle woodlands to arrive at the viaduct again. At this point on the west bank occurred a serious accident when the Stranraer bound mail train became derailed just as it was leaving the viaduct, its coaches crashing down the embankment with some being completely destroyed. Fortunately nobody was injured. No one was sure of the cause but the same engine was involved in another derailment and was promptly dispatched south of the border.

Approaching the site of New Galloway Station, again, the main station building, the sidings and the outline of the platforms can still be seen with the space between them infilled. The buildings to the north of the line have been removed. The main station building, now a private residence stood beside a road bridge over the old line. This bridge was built after the railway opened, as a result of a fatal accident at the spot which resulted in protests about the safety of the then level crossing. Looking under the bridge, the line was visible, stretching out over the

Looking towards Loch Stroan

33

start of the moorland, high on an embankment. Here we began to leave the serenity of the flat rolling meadows of Loch Ken and enter a bleak moorland countryside as the railway wound steadily towards its summit many miles on. After passing through a narrow cutting, the view from the track suddenly opened out with an expansive view over Loch Stroan, which can now be shared by travellers using the Raiders Road. The conifers have done much to lessen the bleakness of the moorland which according to C. H. Dick, writing at the turn of the century, had made some travellers shudder at the desolate view. A four arched granite viaduct took the old railway across the Black-Water-of-Dee before it continued its climb around the boulder strewn side of Airie Hill.

A few miles on Loch Skerrow Halt provided a much needed breather for the hard worked steam trains. For us it provided a suitable spot for lunch as we sat on the concrete platform shaded by a tree, grown large since the railway had departed. The crumpled and twisted remains of the concrete

Loch Skerrow Halt

34

base of the water tower and pump still lay on the other side of the track. The Halt manned by a few hardy souls, whose ruined cottages lay nearby, must have been a lonely place with only the occasional fishing party stopping off. There was no connecting road for many years even after the railway was opened. As we left Loch Skerrow, trees closed in on both sides as the track levelled out for a short time.

The next landmark on the route, the nine arched granite Little Water-of-Fleet viaduct, blown up by the army several years ago, had been removed with hardly a stone left. The walker is now faced with a choice, either to clamber down to the river and attempt to cross it or to detour to the nearby forestry track a couple of hundred metres to the west. At the point where both routes merge, a memorial to a crashed plane was located to the right of the track. Parts of the plane were clearly recognisable as they lay beside the simple memorial to the Polish pilot who was killed piloting his Typhoon south from Ayr. A long straight stretch of the former railway line now used by forestry workers lay ahead as we regained the track. From here the route climbed steadily with good views towards the south, until just before the Big Water-of-Fleet viaduct, where the gradient reversed and the steam train could have taken a welcome breather.

Much has been written about the Big Water-of-Fleet viaduct and despite the first signs of crumbling brickwork its twenty arches of granite strengthened by a cladding of bricks and braced by old rails remained impressive and a local landmark. Repairs to the viaduct were required to cope with the heavy loads carried on the line and it took nearly twenty years to complete them. Amazingly when the viaduct was being built, a boy fell from the top of a crane working on the viaduct and landed eighty feet below, sustaining only two broken ribs. British Rail don't believe that anyone else could be that fortunate and have blocked access to the viaduct by erecting a steel fence. To cross the valley the walker is forced to descend to the valley floor.

The viaduct's connection with John Buchan's book the 39-Steps is, however, an invention of the cinema. The viaduct may have inspired the filmmakers to enable Richard Hannay to make a more dramatic escape from the train, but in the book he gets off at a culvert – the Big Water-of-Fleet viaduct could never be so described. The country surrounding the viaduct forms part of the Cairnsmore-of-Fleet Nature Reserve which consists of a large area of unafforested moorland. The Reserve and Visitor Centre can be accessed from near Gatehouse-of-Fleet Station where a minor road leaves the B796.

Still the route climbed, for a further one-and-a-quarter miles, until its summit was reached at 485 feet. The views were worth the effort. To the right the scene was dominated by the crags of the Clints of Dromore, part of the nature reserve. To the left towards Gatehouse-of-Fleet, nearly six miles away was

Looking towards the Clints of Dromore

a beautiful valley with a road linking the town to the station named after it providing the first link to civilisation for many a mile. The road which was built only after the intervention of an R. Hannay (Robert not Richard) provided an important but slow link from the station to the town. Indeed Gatehouse-of-Fleet Station at six and-a-half miles, held the record for being furthest away from the town it was named after, of any station in Britain. This station was built to placate the aggrieved citizens who had expected the railway to be routed through their town.

The station might hold one claim to fame as it probably was here that Richard Hannay descended from the train on his escape from London. Another curious fact is that beside the station, where today the gate which gives access to the old railway track is located, was situated a converted railway carriage which was used as a church. The railway carriage was no less than one of Queen Victoria's state rail carriages. It was rescued from Portpatrick where it had been abandoned. It was used by the Church of Scotland for services and was broken up on the instructions of the local Kirk Sessions in the 1970's.

The section of the Paddy Line between New Galloway and Gatehouse-of-Fleet Station provides some of the best walking with its dramatic views and its many contrasts. Following the route does open up the beauty of the Galloway and its variety of scenery. Of course no one needs to walk this section in a day, after all, even the steam trains took frequent rests.

Stations and other features (mileage from Dumfries)

C1   Crossmichael Station: 23.5 miles (private residence)
       (84) 729 669

C2   Parton Station: 26.5 miles (private residence – at nearby
       Church is the Maxwell Memorial) (84) 692 701

C3　Loch Ken Viaduct: 27 miles (closed) (84) 684 704

C4　New Galloway Station (Mossdale): 28.5 miles (private residence) (83) 661 705

C5　Loch Stroan Viaduct: 29.5 miles (77) 646 701

C6　Loch Skerrow Halt: 32.5 miles (83) 609 684

C7　Site of Little Water-of-Fleet Viaduct: 34.5 miles (83) 587 671 (now demolished, memorial to crashed plane, 100 yards from the viaduct site)

C8　Big Water-of-Fleet Viaduct: 36.5 miles (closed- part of Cairnsmore-of-Fleet Nature Reserve) (83) 560 644

C9　Gatehouse-of-Fleet Station: 38.5 miles (private residence) (83) 544 624

Journey D

Teapots and Adders

Gatehouse-of-Fleet Station to the site of the Cree Viaduct

Gatehouse-of-Fleet Station

We were standing by the side of the road looking into someone's private garden. The rhododendrons were past their best but otherwise the garden was neat and tidy. It was an oasis of cultivation in the surrounding wilderness. However this was no ordinary garden but the highest station on the now disman- tled 'Paddy Line'. We were at the site of Gatehouse-of-Fleet Station, once a remote outpost of the railway. Here steam trains rested after the steep climb of almost 300 feet from Creetown Station, pausing, before heading inland towards New Gallo- way, ten miles away through some of the most desolate and isolated countryside in Galloway. The Paddy Line contained some of the most scenic views of any railway in Scotland and the section from Gatehouse-of-Fleet Station where the railway emerged from the remote Galloway hills high above Creetown, before racing down to sea level at Palnure beside the Cree Estuary, must be one of the most picturesque. On a clear day the view across to Wigtownshire is dramatic, from Wigtown sitting proud on its hill in the north to the woods near Garlieston in the south. Every twist and turn of the Cree as it nears the sea is laid before you and beyond it in the distance, Newton Stewart the county town.

A need for fresh air, exercise during the Christmas break, and curiosity to trace what remained 30 years after the line had closed brought our group to the crumbling platforms of the station lost in the hills. Accompanying me was my friend Chris, his son Gary and my son, Neil. We were going to trace the course of the disused line as it headed downhill towards Creetown before following the route as far as the River Cree a distance of 12 miles. We were taking the easy route by walking downhill.

It was difficult not to try and imagine what life must have been like when the railway was opened in 1862. Life at remote Gatehouse-of-Fleet Station must have been difficult. This small isolated railway hamlet consisting of the station buildings and some plate layer's cottages was often badly affected by weather. A road to the town it claimed to serve still meant a journey by horse-drawn carriage of over an hour and a lot longer coming back up the hill. Long lonely hours between trains, few passengers and none of the conveniences that we expect today must have made working conditions difficult and probably contributed to the first fatality on the line when the station master at Gatehouse-of-Fleet was struck by a train as he attempted to walk back up from Creetown, having spent the night drinking. There were, however, some advantages with a plentiful supply of peat, although you had to cut it yourself and one enterprising station master even made money by selling sand. An early attempt to close the station in 1951 was rejected, such was the hardship caused to the small hamlet. In those days social reasons were good enough to maintain vital rail links.

We started the walk quickly, since the weather forecast promised little. Already grey clouds were clipping the granite faces of the Clints of Dromore which along with the more distant Cairnsmore-of-Fleet formed a dramatic backdrop to the station. Setting off from the station we headed towards Creetown, the site of the next station on the line, five miles away. Hills to our left blocked the distant view of the Isle of Man but ahead we could see Wigtown Bay with the flat lands of the Machars beyond with the town of Wigtown plainly visible. The route was still clearly defined, the gradient never more than 1 in 80 and comfortable to walk, although steam engines heading the other way must have struggled to reach the summit. Only steam engines were ever used on the Paddy Line which closed in 1965 before diesel units could be introduced. Steam trains could never have found it easy to travel up these gradients. Frequent stops for water to satisfy the thirst of these mechanical monsters were required. Now the sound of these noisy struggles was lost and an eerie silence was all that remained.

A conifer plantation filled the bleak moorland. Inquisitive cows watched as we passed by pausing only for a minute from munching the silage. The gurgling sound of the Moneypool Burn which ran beside the railway for the first two miles could be heard. Otherwise all was quiet.

Two miles from the station we entered a narrow cutting as the road bridge crossed over the line. Here we stopped to search for Hitler's grave, a carving cut out of a coping stone on the bridge by Polish Joe, a stonemason who in 1940 had been working on the bridge, and whose thoughts towards Hitler were summed up in his carving . The carving shows a coffin with

41

Hitler and the date 15.8.40 written underneath was easily found, a small reminder that the war made an impact even in this remote part of Galloway.

Shortly after we reached another cutting known as Rory's Cutting or Teapot Brig which was now used to store silage by the local farmer. To the right of the line on the other side of the road we found 'Teapot Cottage'. In the early days of the railway the appearance of a teapot in the window of the cottage was enough to bring the goods trains to a halt. The train crew knew that this meant whisky was available and many it seemed stopped to partake!

Beyond the 'teapot' was the site of the Culcronchie Viaduct, its four masonry arches which took the railway over the burn of the same name, demolished soon after the line was closed. Here a year ago, on a previous walk, I had a close encounter with an adder. Only the sharp eyes of my son who shouted a warning stopped me from stepping on its coiled form. The adder seemed just as surprised as I was. Quickly I had stepped back and we appeared to eye each other before it slipped

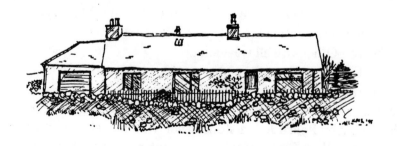

Teapot Cottage

away, but not before I captured it on film from a safe distance! My friends were not so keen to walk with me after that, since this was the second time in a few months that I had almost stepped on an adder. My other encounter was at Loch Grannoch a few miles inland. Walk carefully in the Galloway Hills! Watching our footsteps we walked to the nearby road before picking up the route at the other side of the demolished viaduct.

Between here and Creetown Station the threatened rain began but never became more than a drizzle. Creetown Station at Spittal Lennies lies about half-a-mile from the small town separated from it by the now strongly flowing Moneypool Burn.

Sadly the station, whose name probably means 'the meadow beside a hospital' or more appropriately a meeting place for travellers has been used as a coal yard since its closure and was in a poor state the ticket office crumbling away and the drainage system having packed in flooding the area between the platforms.

At this station occurred one of the most serious accidents on the line when a goods train crashed into the afternoon Castle Douglas to Stranraer train. The crew of the goods train who had been imbibing at an hotel in Crossmichael had ignored the signals and carried on towards the station. No one was killed but the driver of the goods train took fright and ran away. The fireman and guard stayed and were dismissed!

Creetown Station nestling as it does at the bottom of a steep hill was an important stop for the steam trains to pick up water. However there was an early dispute over the cost of supplying water from the local estate. Twenty pounds a year was demanded and only ten pounds offered. The railway made efforts to relocate their water tower at Newton Stewart but with limited success. Some arrangement must have been reached as the photographs that I have seen of Creetown Station show a water tower. The problems with water were to contribute to a further incident near Creetown Station.

Galloway enjoys a mild climate but occasionally as in 1895, 1940 and 1996 the weather conspired to deposit a lot of snow on the area causing great disruption. Bad weather led to an incident during the big sna' of 1895 when drifts of over 20 feet were recorded, and many areas in Galloway were cut off for days. A train became stuck outside Creetown Station having failed to make it up the bank from Palnure. The passengers knowing that the station was not far away were not too bothered, but after an hour and several attempts to walk to the station the passengers knew that they were trapped. They were told that a snow plough was on its way. Eventually many hours late the snow plough arrived but was of no use its water supply having been used up in the struggle to get there. There was water available at Creetown but no one on the railway wanted to use it for fear of being charged extra. A lesson for those seeking to privatise water! Some passengers stayed in Creetown

Graddoch Viaduct

when the train was able to restart; others who chose to stay on were less fortunate as the train again broke down at Rory's Cutting. Its not known if anything warming was offered from the teapot. It was three days later before the passengers reached their destinations.

Fortunately for us the weather had improved and with the sun setting low gave a luminous quality to the scene. The line now took a sharp turn as we headed along the Cree valley passing through several shallow cuttings before entering attractive woods. The Cairnsmore or Graddoch viaduct which consisted of eight sandstone arches several of which had been demolished proved no obstacle as we easily descended from the banking to the road which leads to the impressive Cairnsmore Lodge and onwards to the top of Cairnsmore-of-Fleet.

The railway which was now carried on an embankment stretched out in front of us the Palnure Bridge quickly reached as light began to fade. The railway bridge over the A75 had long been taken down but we climbed the embankment on the other side to continue our trail determined to reach the Cree. Palnure Station which closed in 1951 almost seemed untouched by the years. Now a private residence the buildings had been well maintained but little remained of the sidings.

The line now headed straight for the River Cree a mile further on. There we stopped at the river with its muddy banks proving too big an obstacle to cross with only rotting timbers projecting above the water line. It was hard to imagine that trains hurtled across here, often at speeds of 60mph, preparing to tackle the slopes in front of them. Risks must have been taken and on track which was often criticised for poor maintenance one engine lost all its carriages derailed at this point, due to a broken coupling. The engine reached Palnure before the driver and fireman were aware.

Nowadays the traveller along the Paddy Line has to walk,

but that hasn't spoiled the views; indeed there is more time to enjoy this tranquil part of Scotland. As we waited to cross the busy A75 to reach our car for the journey home we wondered if many of the travellers hurtling along the road were even aware that this region once boasted of an alternative form of transport which might have taken some of the pressure off the busy roads.

Stations and other features (mileage from Dumfries)

D1 Gatehouse-of-Fleet Station: 38.5 miles
(private residence) (83) 544 624

D2 Site of "Hitler's Grave" on road bridge over the railway:
40.5 miles (83) 515 616

D3 Teapot Cottage: 41 miles (private residence)
(83) 512 612

D4 Site of Culcronchie Viaduct: 41.25 miles (demolished)
– **beware of adders!** (83) 566 613

D5 Creetown Station (Spittal Lennies): 43.5 miles
(83) 476 600

D6 Graddoch Viaduct: 45.5 miles (partly demolished)
(83) 462 631

D7 Palnure Bridge: 46 miles(closed) (83) 455 634

D8 Palnure Station: 46.25 miles (private residence)
(83) 452 634

D9 Site of Cree Viaduct: 47.25 miles (demolished)
(83) 436 635

Journey E

The Railway Through the Machars

The Machars that broad peninsula of land between Luce and Wigtown bays, already had a railway, the Portpatrick Railway which ran along its northern boundary, but there was demand for another railway to link with the PPR and allow the agricultural produce of this fertile region to reach new markets. The first part of the line, opened to Wigtown in 1875 and was easy to build on fairly flat land and with no major engineering works. Costs, however, increased as the River Bladnoch was crossed and the railway reached south towards Whithorn. Gradients were steeper as the railway twisted and weaved its way through as many small communities as it could. The railway finally stretched from Newton Stewart, where it branched from the PPR to Whithorn a distance of just over 19 miles.

Creameries were built alongside the railway at Whithorn, Sorbie and Bladnoch and provided much needed income. enabling a steady flow of dairy produce to the new markets in the north of England. Day excursions to the Isle of Man from Garlieston, provided an alternative source of revenue during a short summer season. The railway struggled to survive and did not remain independent for long and in 1885 it merged with the PPR to form the Portpatrick and Wigtownshire Railway (PPW).

My son Neil and I started our exploration of the railway through the Machars at the site of Whithorn Station, over thirty years after it had closed to all traffic and over forty-five years after it carried its last passenger.

With the discovery of the remains of possibly the oldest Christian settlements in Scotland at Whithorn, the town is attracting many pilgrims seeking to discover about the life of the early Christian saint, St Ninian. Few would notice nowadays,

47

that the village ever had a railway connection, although any pilgrims slaking their thirst at the 'Railway Inn' must wonder about its name. As you would expect little exists of what was once the most southerly station in Scotland. The modest station buildings and extensive sidings have gone replaced by a newly built fire-station and a bus garage. The SCWS Creamery with its tall chimney had also gone. Between the two the route of the disused line slipped out of Whithorn, almost unnoticed into the countryside.

The first few miles of the track pass through typical Machars countryside, with its undulating hills and strong agricultural traditions. Black bags of hay frequently provided obstacles as the farmers had discovered a convenient place for storage. Within half-a-mile of leaving Whithorn, the highest point on the line had been reached and from there the line lost height until it reached Millisle Station, four miles on. Heading towards Whithorn, it was a steady climb for a steam train. A gatekeepers house at the level crossing at Chapel Outon a couple of miles on was the first sign of the railway touching habitation. The house was still standing although in a bad state of disrepair. It must have been a lonely task with few trains and only a scattering of farms around.

Level Crossing at Chapel Outon

The next stretch of the route was overgrown and the walker is forced to walk beside the track until Broughton Skeog where there was another level crossing. This site once boasted a wooden platform and a water tower to satisfy the thirst of steam trains climbing the gradient towards Whithorn. A siding to collect the milk urns was also constructed which shows how hard the railway fought for what must have been scant business. The walker is rewarded by finding himself in quiet countryside away from the main roads able to enjoy the tranquil peace of the Machars.

The walk continued over a couple of intact railway bridges before our luck ran out and we reached the abutments of a missing bridge over a drainage ditch. We found a fallen tree to crawl across otherwise we faced a detour to continue the journey. On the other side, once reached, the line continued and on the east side the boundary wall of Galloway House was glimpsed as the route approached Garlieston. Near Pouton Farm, the last farm before Millisle Station, conditions became more difficult when we encountered the twin perils of walking disused railway lines, when first the route passed through a deep cutting in which the drainage had broken down leaving the route waterlogged, and then as the rail bridge over the B7052, Garlieston to Sorbie road was approached a bramble entangled embankment forced us down to the nearby field.

We had almost reached the site of the next station on the line, near the coastal village of Garlieston. This village, with less than seven hundred souls in 1875, could boast of two stations. When first the railway reached Garlieston its terminus was near Millisle farm about a mile from the harbour. There was a clamour for a branch line to connect with the harbour to encourage both the fairly extensive coastal trading and lucrative tourist excursions to the Isle of Man.

Within a year, with local support, the line had been

constructed from the original station into the village and a new station had been built. Inevitably there was an initial problem with naming the stations. The original one being called in turn Garliestown Passenger Station, Garliestown Upper, Garliestown Junction, Millisle Junction and then finally Millisle. The harbour station was known as Garliestown New, Garliestown Village and then Garliestown and from the turn of the century Garlieston.

The route taken by this short branch could still be traced. Looking towards Garlieston from the site of Millisle Station a ridge could be seen crossing the field. This was the route taken by the railway which then ran parallel to the road leading into the village. This part was an impenetrable jungle of brambles and we had to use the road. The railway then cut across the road and clung to the boundary of Galloway House eventually reaching the site of the station, now a park. The village once had a grain store, evidence of its trading past, which now is used by the Wigtown Bay Trading Post which literally sells anything, with a wide range of new and secondhand goods. Trains had the option of going beyond the station onto the harbour to unload goods and passengers. One memorable photograph I saw, showed day trippers herded in open cattle trucks speeding towards Garlieston.

Trains were frequently too long and often had difficulty unloading at the short station platforms. A further problem with Garlieston was that the harbour is tidal and if the tide was missed there was a long wait before the boat could get in.

Returning to the site of Millisle Station clear signs of its railway past could still be seen. The station house was now a private residence with the space between the platforms now used for drying clothes. An island platform was constructed at Millisle, the only one on the line, and with the building of the line to Whithorn, a shuttle service was run to Garlieston. The signal box to the west of the station has long been removed but a careful observer can still trace the line of the tracks and sidings. The railway then ran west, climbing slowly towards the next station at Sorbie a distance of two miles. A deep ditch required a detour as we left the cutting which led from Millisle Station and beyond that much of the line had been reclaimed by farming, but the views especially of the hills to the north were worthwhile. The Sorbie Tower, an impressive ruin, the ancestral home of the Hannay Clan, could be seen in woods to the north of the former railway route and made a pleasant short detour from the old railway.

As the line approached Sorbie Station another missing bridge held up progress briefly, before the station which is about half a mile to the north of the village was reached. The scene had been totally transformed with the A746 realigned to run in front of the former station building. The line taken by the old road was behind the station buildings and parts still remain. The road bridge over the railway had gone and a garage rested in the space. The changes, however, were even more extensive. Originally a creamery stood alongside the station buildings with its own siding. These buildings were demolished and a new creamery built a hundred yards to the east. It was this creamery that we passed as we approached the station. Also, now closed, milk tankers stood in the forecourt exchanging milk collected from nearby farms. Never was the dominance of road over rail so completely captured as in that scene.

Beyond Sorbie Station the route, still heading east, continued to climb exchanging rich farmlands for rocky pastures. Walking was not too easy as Whauphill Station was reached with the line overgrown. This village was the nearest point to Port William on the west coast and horsedrawn carriages carried passengers between the two at the turn of the century. The engine shed and platform remained.

The route now turned north-east as the railway rolled

down towards Kirkinner but while the scenery was attractive the walking was difficult with missing bridges and bramble entangled embankments. Modern houses obscured the former railway's entrance into the village. This station once boasted two sidings and a loading bay along with a single platform. The site is now part of a field with what looks like part of the platform left isolated. I found it difficult to work out what the station layout must have looked like. Beyond the station, however, it was easy to trace the line towards Bladnoch River. The railway reached the river on an embankment which shielded Baldoon Mains with its airfields, important during the war, from the main road. Then at the site of another creamery complete with siding, the railway crossed the Bladnoch over two iron lattice girders

Bladnoch Bridge

supported by a central pillar of whinstone. The metal work had been removed from what was the biggest and most expensive engineering project on the line. It was the second time that the

52

river had been crossed by the railways. Upriver the Bladnoch had been bridged near to Kirkcowan by the Portpatrick Railway.

The village of Bladnoch with its history of whisky production, nestled at the foot of the hill on which Wigtown is built overlooking Wigtown Bay. The appropriately named Windyhill monument a memorial to the covenantors, and the tower of the town hall are landmarks for miles around which mean that although Wigtown is small it is never likely to be unnoticed. Sensibly the railway builders built their route around the hill and the station lay to the south of the town, carefully chosen for its access to the harbour and its gentler gradients to the town centre than a station built further north. The platform is still intact but while all the buildings have been razed to the ground the foundations can still be traced.

Ahead under a road bridge lay a narrow cutting. As the cutting was flooded and polluted by petrol we had to carefully work our way along until we came out at the site of the Martyr's Stake. The embankment had been turned into a path leading to the stone pillar which marks the site a few yards out on the moss. So many gave their lives for religious freedom in Galloway and one can only imagine the resolute faith of those willing to drown slowly for their faith.

Moving on we reached a wooden hide for studying the variety of birds on Wigtown Sands. The open views towards Cairnsmore-of-Fleet and across the bay to Creetown made us realise that the next stretch of the railway was across flat land. We picked up on the track near West Kirkland Farm and were making good progress until we reached the site of a missing bridge over Borrowmoss Burn. We were forced to make a long detour to a nearby road to reach the other side of this deep burn. Progress towards the site of the former level crossing at Carslae was steady and even through the woods to the north the path of the former railway could be followed easily.

At Carsegowan we reached the site of a munitions factory, long derelict but which along with the similar site we encountered at Edingham near Dalbeattie had contributed to Galloway's war effort and given added importance to the railway network in the area. The buildings cover a considerable area and must have used a large number of people.

Beyond Carsegowan where the railway crossed under the A714 was Causewayend, which once boasted of a wooden platform, sidings and a water tower. The road had been re-routed to the west leaving the former road bridge stranded. Signs of the siding were still there but the next rail bridge was missing, forcing another detour. From here on the route passed through rich pasture and much use has been made of the line by the farmers for storage. We passed the site of the last level crossing at Mains of Penninghame which once also boasted of a wooden platform. The route thereafter was flat until nearing the road at Barwhirran Croft when, like a siege ramp, the railway climbed rapidly towards the bridge over the road. This part was entangled and overgrown and we found it easier to pick up on the far side of the bridge. The surrounding land changed quickly from farmland to moorland within a few hundred yards. Now it was a steady climb until the line had levelled off nearer to Newton Stewart which was now only a couple of miles away. The countryside with its outcrops of rocks was peaceful, with animals grazing undisturbed. We even startled two foxes, who froze for a moment and then bolted.

At Moor Park of Barr we passed under the last road bridge and saw the final stretch of the former railway ahead. As we neared the A75 the line started to disappear, eventually becoming only a narrow raised ridge in the fields. It was as if someone had rubbed the line away. By the time we arrived at the A75 the railway had gone with the widening A75 having removed all trace. On the Newton Stewart side of the A75 the line can only be seen as it nears the road bridge approaching the station. The line had finally left the Machars – it would never return.

Beyond Moor Park of Barr

Stations and other features (mileage from Whithorn)

E1 Whithorn Station: 0 miles (83) 446 408
E2 Broughton Skeog: 2.6 miles (83) 455 441
E3 Garlieston Station: 2.9 miles (1 mile from Millisle)
(83) 478 461
E4 Millisle: 3.9 miles (83) 465 464
E5 Sorbie Tower: 4.9 miles (83) 451 471
E6 Sorbie Station: 5.9 miles (83) 435 477
E7 Whauphill Station: 8.2 miles (83) 405 499
E8 Kirkinner Station: 9.8 miles (83) 421 517
E9 Bladnoch Bridge:11.2 miles (demolished) (83) 424 541
E10 Wigtown Station: 12.2 miles (83) 434 548
E11 Martyrs' Stake: 12.4 miles (83) 437 557
E12 Causewayend: 15.5 miles (83) 422 596 (near site of
former Carsegowan Munitions Works)
E13 Newton Stewart Station: 19.1 miles (83) 405 649

Journey F

The End of the Line

From the Cree to Challoch Junction

It was reported that when the last train left Newton Stewart Station the crowds remained until they heard it rumbling over the Cree Viaduct way down in the valley. Today the viaduct is no more, the rotting wooden stumps were just visible above the mudflats in the river. This was the depressing scene at the start of the last section of our walk along the Paddy Line, from the Cree Viaduct to Challoch Junction where the 'Port Road' had been joined by that late interloper the Girvan and Portpatrick Junction Railway. In the absence of the viaduct we had to backtrack from Newton Stewart where we were camping, to start our walk.

The Cree Bridge crossed the River Cree just before it broadened into an estuary. There were problems with its construction, when a high tide and thick floating ice caused damage to the wooden pillars on which sat the three girder spans.

It was a fair climb back to Newton Stewart as the track, high on an embankment, at first, reached the Newton Stewart to Wigtown road. No wonder the trains hurtled across the viaduct with the momentum built up on this short downhill section. Rerouting of the road has removed any traces of the road bridge but the disused track was soon seen high on the far side as the route reached towards Newton Stewart. The view over the town, back to the far hills, with Cairnsmore-of-Fleet again dominating and then down to the Cree Estuary was outstanding. Due to the building of the bypass around Newton Stewart there was no sign of the rail bridge over the A75 and the walker is forced to climb down to road level to enter the town. Once a rail centre, where the branch line to Whithorn left, Newton Stewart has succeeded like Castle Douglas in removing the railways from its memory. The proud facade of the old station remains, now used as a post office sorting office, but behind the entrance all has changed. Gone was the island platform, an attractive feature, and the platform behind the booking office. This area, now being used as an industrial estate has retained only an engine shed. To the west of the station where the branch line diverged, there was another engine shed pressed into alternative uses. As a prime site in a town surrounded by hills and fields the station's fate was secured, when the railway closed.

The depressing picture continued as farmers had ploughed in any signs of the route as it left Newton Stewart. The track reappeared at the road bridge to West Knockbrex, just beyond the Christian Centre at High Burbuchany and continued for the next mile to the site of the next rail bridge over the A75. Beyond that, for several miles, the route of the disused line has been absorbed by the realignment of the A75 or hidden in woods which run beside the road. Of the bridge over the River Bladnoch nothing remained and just when you feel that the route has gone forever, it reappeared where the A735 crossed over the old line on the approach to Kirkcowan. From here to Kirkcowan, the route taken by the line was visible but largely choked by the inevitable gorse, brambles and nettles – potent obstacles preventing quick progress even at times, blocking views of the church tower which dominated the village.

At Kirkcowan we stopped for lunch having seen a lot of the A75 and little of the route and were hoping for an improvement after a break. Two further road bridges crossed the former railway as the line passed through Kirkcowan, the cutting in-between impenetrable, as we headed towards the site of the station which was to the west of the village. No buildings remained, but the platforms which were still largely intact and gave a good indication of the layout. From here, it looked as if the route was clear as we headed towards Glenluce Station. Our optimism was illfounded, as we reached yet another missing bridge, this time over a minor road. We forced our way down to the road only to face on the other side a sinister looking black burn. We decided to walk to the nearby B733, crossed the burn by the road bridge and worked our way back to the route of the former railway.

Just when we felt like giving up, and the stretch from Newton Stewart did test our resolve, the route began to improve and with the welcome relief of the Tarff Bridge being intact, good progress was made and soon we once again reached the A75.

We walked along the A75 for a short distance before we located the disused line as it crossed Dergoals Moss on the far side. Built on an embankment, which must have been a considerable feat, given the marshy conditions, we headed towards Glenluce. It has to be said that the Ordnance Survey map let us down, as it missed out many features such as bridges and cuttings, making it difficult to know how close we were to the last station on our walk. Much remained of the route at this point and the walking was good apart from one missing bridge which we managed to get across by crawling along a pole over the burn. The conditions suffered by the navvies building this part must have been difficult, and probably contributed to one of the few scenes of unrest when the line was being built, when a gang of workers led by two leaders picked on some of the foremen, viciously attacking them. They were caught and jailed in Stranraer.

The rail route slipped into Glenluce passing the backs of the houses in this pretty village. Again the Station was to the west just beyond a road bridge. Little remained – the space between the platforms having been filled in long ago. Houses were being built a little further along the line making it difficult to picture what the station must have been like.

Beyond Glenluce Station was a picturesque graveyard, another road bridge and then the jewel in the crown - the Glenluce Viaduct. Once the A75 wound a tortuous route through its pillars, now the opening of the bypass has left the viaduct stranded over a road leading nowhere. A sad situation, for such an impressive structure.

We crossed the viaduct pushing on towards Challoch Junction where the Port Road was joined by the railway from Girvan. The route passed through pleasant woods which concealed the height of the embankment we were walking along. Again one can only admire the navvies who laboured to build this railway and the constructions they achieved with little more than shovels and picks. Emerging from the woods, the line became overgrown and so close to the junction, we were forced to side-step to the nearby field. Ahead we could see the end of our journey, as we spotted emerging from the hills to the north, rusty rails gleaming in the sun. The sound of gunfire provided a suitable backdrop as we closed the gap, the gunners at the nearby firing range unaware of their good timing. A final missing bridge and we were there. The present line has been realigned but the junction is still clear. After almost sixty miles we could see rails again.

Of course the Girvan line was not built until after the Port Road had been completed, and there was the inevitable conflict between the two railways, but it has survived and taken sole mastery of the rails from here to Stranraer. As we headed back to Glenluce we saw our first train. I wondered how long that sight would remain. How many miles was it to Girvan?

Stations and other features (mileages from Dumfries)

F1 Newton Stewart Station: 49.5 miles (83) 405 650
F2 Upper Bladnoch Bridge: 54 miles (demolished)
         (84) 342 629
F3 Kirkcowan Station: 58 miles (83) 323 610
F4 Tarff Bridge: 60.2 miles (83) 296 597
F5 Glenluce Station: 64.5 miles (82) 196 574
F6 Glenluce Viaduct: 64.8 miles (82) 192 573
F7 Challoch Junction: 66.7 miles (83) 169 570

Journey G

Down to the Sea

From Stranraer to Portpatrick

The building of the Port Road did not turn out as intended. Portpatrick, a picturesque seaside village was the site chosen for the train to connect with the ferry to Ireland. The journey from Portpatrick to Donaghadee is just twenty-one miles and was the shortest sea-crossing between Galloway and Ireland. Unfortunately Portpatrick is on the exposed west coast, where even on a calm day waves can pound the harbour. While the crossing from Stranraer, which was in the sheltered Loch Ryan, to Larne was longer, it was less likely to be affected by the weather and had the benefit of a safe anchorage. Engineers had doubted for many years whether Portpatrick could ever be made suitable for use as a ferry terminus, but the government had continued to finance the development of the harbour which had been used in the past to ferry troops to Ireland and to carry the royal mail, although the mail service had been stopped in 1849.

There was also problems with constructing the railway. The gradient profile for the line looked like a hill. A steep rise from Stranraer a summit near Colfin Station and then an even steeper drop towards Portpatrick where the station could only be reached by a deep cutting through solid rock. From the station after difficult manoeuvres due to a short trailing junction, there was a branch to the harbour which could only be operated by a train and four wagons at a time. There was literally no room for expansion.

The line to Portpatrick was officially opened in 1862 almost eighteen months after trains had run to Stranraer and a ferry service had been in operation between Stranraer and

61

Larne. The trouble was that there was no steamer service at Portpatrick to carry the mails to Ireland, as it had been discontinued. Work on the harbour had not progressed and even on its opening day the line to Portpatrick had been effectively relegated to the role of a small branch railway. Attempts were made to establish a regular ferry between Portpatrick and Donaghadee but they failed and the harbour branch finally closed in 1875 with the harbour platform being dismantled and the paving slabs used to enlarge the station at Newton Stewart. The harbour branch had never apparently been used by passengers who had had to commute from the high station to the harbour.

We started the walk in Stranraer having travelled by train from Ayr on an almost empty train, an ominous sign for the future of this line, and been deposited at the Stranraer Harbour Station. We walked back to the site of Stranraer Town where the line to Portpatrick had departed. The station was still in use but only by railway engineers, the station having been closed to the public in 1966. It was well maintained but surrounded by empty engine sheds. A double set of tracks swept into the station but merged just beyond the platform and then stopped at a set of rusty buffers a few yards on.

The first road bridge over the former line was infilled and our walk quickly became one of spot the railway as a hospital and then an industrial estate had been built on the line of the track removing all traces of the former line. However, the route taken by the line was picked up as we walked along the A77 heading out of town. From near a farm at the site of a missing bridge the line was possible to walk along, with care until the abutment of the next missing bridge where the line had crossed the A77. On the far side of the road, the track began to climb along the side of a hill. The uphill climb had begun. The track, a shallow cutting, was a tangle of gorse and bramble. We kept to the side of the track, making steady progress past the site of a missing bridge at Whiteley's Farm before the line entered another deep and impenetrable cutting. We were forced to keep to the high ground to the side of the cutting being rewarded by the views back towards Stranraer and to the east. In many ways the view summed up why there had been so many changes and closures on this stretch. We could identify the woods which blocked our view of Glenluce with its station, Challoch Hill where the railway swept round to the north, Dunragit Station, Castle Kennedy Station and in Stranraer both the Harbour and Town Stations. Five stations within eight miles, with only one now open. There was too small a population to require this level of service. Connecting them all was the A75 with a busy stream of traffic heading to and from the ferry terminal at Stranraer.

Our depression at the state of the line was lifted as we reached the site of the now demolished Piltanton Viaduct. The line was clearly visible on an embankment as it snaked across the

Site of Piltanton Viaduct

flat shallow valley which contained Piltanton Burn. None of the thirteen brick arches on masonry piles survived, but the burn, a modest obstacle was quickly overcome and after a brief climb, the embankment on the far side was reached. One further missing bridge over a minor road led to a long cutting. Emerging from it, we could spot the village of Lochans down the hill on our left the biggest centre of population on the route to Portpatrick which the railway had managed to miss. The view to the east now took in Luce bay and the military airfield at West Freugh with its distinctive golf ball radar.

We then reached a viaduct crossing the road leading down towards Duchra farm. The first arches were intact but the last one was missing bringing us to a sudden stop and forcing us to retrace our steps down to the nearby field. We rejoined the track near an attractive wooden overbridge close to Cairnpat Farm. Here the railway ran parallel to the road and several times we used it to miss out a boggy section or a bramble filled cutting. Still the railway climbed not yet having reached the summit or

Viaduct over minor road from Duchra Farm

the first station. Road realignment proved confusing but the track was picked up now on the far side of the A77. Stretches of good walking were interspersed with harder sections of winding through gorse bushes.

With the transmitter on Cairn Pat Hill to our right, the track at last showed signs of levelling out after four miles of a steady climb. Ahead lay Colfin Station overshadowed by the now closed creamery which had kept the line open as far as here, at least for freight, until 1959. There was evidence of sidings to the east as we approached the station. The platform was to the right hand side complete with greenhouse and stables! Behind the stables was the creamery, parts of which were used at present as a store for carpets and another part as a smokehouse. Beyond what had been a level crossing was the station house. Where were the people who would have used this station? There was no village closeby and even the farm after which the station was named was one and a half miles away.

After the station the line to Portpatrick started its descent gently at first and then more steeply. More unusual obstacles lay ahead, as near Lagganmore Golf and Country Club a garden had been laid out along the line and then a golf course. The ninth green covered the site of the track and further on over a bridge made up of old railway sleepers which seemed appropriate, was the seventh green. The transformation was complete, with the inclines which confronted the golfers not as demanding as those which faced the train drivers.

The sea lay ahead and beyond Ireland. We reached an extensive caravan site which straddled the railway line with an impressive three arched viaduct crossing a minor road. Land next to the railway had been levelled and used for siting caravans and so it was difficult to tell if there had been sidings. Portpatrick was still hidden to the north. Dunskey Castle dominated the view in front and beyond steep cliffs. You began to wonder if the railway would disappear into the sea, when a steep turn to the right led into a deep and narrow cutting with rocky sides. A wooden footbridge, part of the path to Dunskey Castle crossed a narrow gap, known as Tailor's Peak on the seaward side of the cutting, which must have added to the difficulties of the trains trying to climb a gradient of 1 in 57 by adding crosswinds to the steepness of the climb. Through the cutting the track emerged above the village, with a large hotel commanding the cliffs to the north of the village and above the attractive seaside resort. Across the North Channel the chimney of the Belfast Power Station could be seen. The track taken by the former railway continued to descend, first behind a new primary school then under a partially filled in road bridge, through a narrow cutting and then straight into a block of flats, built in the last few years on the site of the station. Steep banks arose on two sides of the station site increasing the impression of limited space in which once was crammed an engine shed, stone water tower and the station buildings. Part of the platform complete with station

Dunskey Castle

master's house remained but nothing else. The station lay some distance from the main village when it was built.

Trains waiting to go onto the harbour branch could not go straight through but required to be shunted onto the trailing junction. Due to the limited space only four wagons could go down the harbour branch at one time. 'Go down', seemed appropriate, with a gradient of 1 in 35! Only the abutments of the bridge over the main road remained as the rest of the iron girder bridge has long ago been dismantled and the embankment which carried the harbour branch has been removed. The site of the terminus itself, was now also landscaped and used as tennis courts.

We walked down to the sea, a matter of yards from the tennis courts. This day the waves gently lapped the rocky shore with Ireland prominent on the horizon. The journey had been a long one, over eighty miles from its start in Dumfries. The Port Road should have stopped here at the harbour but that never was a practical reality. The gradients, the lack of space, the problems with the harbour ensured that this railway was going to be sidelined by the superior claims of Stranraer as a ferry port. Portpatrick did, however, add a lot of political intrigue to the history of Scotland to Ireland crossings.

I had left this walk to the last, believing wrongly that most of the track was unwalkable. While it did have its difficult parts, the walk was worthwhile, as the line which crossed the Rhinns of Galloway brought with it the reward of magnificent views. _ The building of the line must have appeared to many as a Victorian folly, and while it only briefly achieved the purpose for which it was constructed, as a branch line, it brought pleasure to many who simply wanted to spend a day at the seaside.

Stations and other features (mileage from Dumfries)

G1   Stranraer Town Station: 73 miles (82) 066 604

G2   Piltanton Viaduct: 75.5 miles (demolished) (82) 058 575

G3   Colfin Station: 77.5 miles (private residence)
       (82) 038 547

G4   Dunskey Castle: 80.2 miles (82) 004 534

G5   Portpatrick Station: 80.5 miles (demolished)
       (82) 003 543

G6   End of harbour branch: 80.8 miles (now tennis courts)
       (82) 996 542

Postscript

Nowadays the only railway which runs into Galloway is the line from Girvan to Stranraer. The short freight line from Dumfries to Maxwelltown, at the eastern end of the former Port Road, is strictly speaking in Dumfriesshire.

The first railway to close was Portpatrick harbour branch in 1873 but then that decision was political, based on the Government's decision not to develop Portpatrick as the ferry terminal. At the time of this closure the railway network in Galloway was still expanding with both the completion of the Wigtownshire railway extension to Whithorn and the line from Girvan to Challoch Junction still almost four years away.

The railways underwent reorganisation when the Wigtownshire and Portpatrick Railways merged in 1876 to form the Portpatrick and Wigtownshire Railways (PPW). The PPW was jointly run by the Caledonian Railway and the Glasgow and South-Western Railway (G&SWR). The G&SWR also ran the other railways in the area. The Garlieston branch was the first casualty this century when it closed to passenger traffic on the 1st March 1903. There were no further changes until after the First World War when as part of the general reorganisation of the railways the lines in the area became part of the London Midland and Scottish Railway Group (LMS) in 1923.

The Second World War meant that the railways were kept busy and even saw the opening of a new branch for military purposes with the completion of the Cairnryan Railway in 1943. Cairnryan, six miles north of Stranraer on the east coast of Loch Ryan, was developed as an emergency port, if the Clyde ports or Liverpool had been closed due to bombing. The line was built as single track and left the main line one mile east of Stranraer Harbour Junction. The line was six miles long and despite attempts by the local authority to keep it open was closed by the early 1960s.

The rundown of the railways in Galloway really began after nationalisation in 1948 when the railways became part of the Scottish region of British Railways. The line to Portpatrick closed to passengers on the 6th February 1950 and a similar fate befell the Wigtownshire branch the same year on the 25th September. Freight services, however did continue as far as Colfin Station until 16th May 1959 and to Whithorn until the 5th October 1964. The Kirkcudbright Branch lost its passenger service on the 3rd May 1965 and on the 14th June 1965 the railway was closed between Maxwelltown and Challoch Junction. Hope remained for a couple of years that the Port Road might be reopened as the rails were not lifted. Hope turned to despair with the lifting of the rails. The Stewartry of Kirkcudbright was left without a railway and Wigtownshire with a link only to the north. The dismantling of a once proud railway network was almost completed. Only time will tell if Galloway will one day become a train free zone.

Bibliography

The **books** that I found most useful were:

Rails To Portpatrick:
  H D Thorne, T Stephenson & Sons Ltd*
The Little Railways of South-West Scotland:
  D L Smith, David and Charles*
The Portpatrick and Wigtownshire Railways:
  C E J Fryer, Oakwood Press
British Railways - Past and Present No 19 South-West Scotland:
  K Sanders & D Hodgins, Silver Link Publishing
The Glasgow and South-Western Railway, 1850-1923:
  Stephenson Locomotive Society*
Regional History of the Railways of Great Britain, Volume 6, Scotland, The Lowlands and The Borders:
  John Thomas, David St. John Thomas
Scottish Railway Walks:
  M E Ellison, Cicerone Press
Monuments and Moorlands:
  Peter D Starling, Wigtown District Museum Service .
Causewayend to Castle-Douglas:
  Alistair Penman, Forward Press, Castle Douglas
Dalbeattie & District In Bygone Days:
  Dalbeattie Museum

*Some of these books are difficult to obtain. GC Book Publishers Ltd., Wigtown may be able to help.

Other sources of information were local museums: Stewartry Museum, Kirkcudbright, Dalbeattie Museum and Newton Stewart Museum. The Carnegie Library, Ayr was also a useful source of information.

Ordnance Survey Maps used were numbers 82, 83 and 84

THE LOST RAILWAY LINES OF GALLOWAY

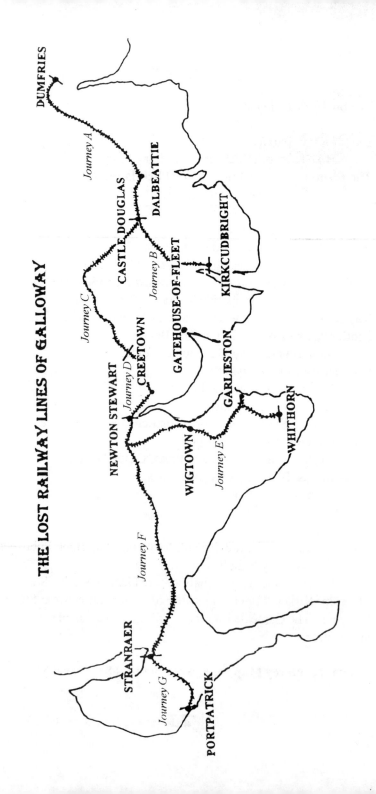